the immeasurable fold

the immeasurable fold

selected poems 2000–2015

luke kurtis

the immeasurable fold: selected poems 2000–2015

a luke kurtis/bd-studios.com production
Published by bd-studios.com in New York City, 2018
Copyright © 2018 by luke kurtis

Design and drawings by luke kurtis

ISBN 978-0-9992078-3-3

All Rights Reserved. No part of this publication may be reproduced, stored in a retrieval system or transmitted in any form or by any means without the prior permission in writing of copyright holders and of the publisher.

Pages 129–130 constitute an extension of the copyright page.

contents

introduction 9

the immeasurable fold 13
execution 15
spelunking 17
old clothes 20
ode to my roots 21
tempest 26
mary 28
marie was an artist 33
lament over home 37
moment 40
cherokee hills 44
confederate rose 48
love in the mourning 51
lazy dreams 58

ghazal	60
the sound (which is more alarming?)	62
suspension	64
sink	66
shadows we shall be	69
detained	71
angel be my guide	73
onewaytripup	75
are there?	77
heaven's sun so bright	80
when the zephyr came a'calling	83
cold congregation	84
ascension	87
the agony of betrayal	91

battlefields	93
autoatomicanxiety	96
sad american night (for Jack Kerouac)	100
forever	102
have and have not	106
falling sweetly upon	107
precipice	108
the causes of civilization	109
vigil and bold	111
everlasting	115
carried	119
the waking	121
theodora	122
finished	126
about the poems and drawings	129
about the artist	131

introduction

This is my second book. Well, not exactly, but sort of. Let me explain…

I published my first book in 2000. *like an angel dead in your arms* was a collection of my earliest poems, written from 1995 to 1999. I was eager to prepare my second collection and soon compiled a manuscript of new poems, all written in 2000, titled *lazy dreams and other memories*. I submitted the manuscript to a few publishers and, like almost all of my poetry submissions even to this day, it was rejected.

Fast forward a few years to 2005. My creative work had come to emphasize the visual but poetry still remained a part of my practice. As I prepared my first art exhibition, I decided to include some of the poems from that unpublished manuscript. I even repurposed the title and also published a small catalog of the show—poetry, photography, and digital collage.

After that, the manuscript became hidden away in my files, but eventually I revisited it. As I read the poems for the first time in many years, I was fascinated with the inner life they depicted. In many ways these old poems felt very far removed. Yet the poems provide important context to my life. Simply stated: I would not be who I am today without the experiences they chronicled. Yet, of course, with so many years having passed, they now told only a small part of the story. It was a story that I wanted to tell, but it needed to be extended to give a fuller picture of my life. So that is what I set out to do.

the immeasurable fold is the result. Here I have compiled the most relevant and best poems from the original *lazy dreams* manuscript along with select poems from the following fifteen years. All together this collection spans a decade and a half of my life.

It's hard to believe I've been writing poetry for over twenty years. But somehow I have. The wheel of time keeps turning, and the muses keep pushing me on. And while some things have changed immensely, others have not. I recently compiled another poetry manuscript of work written mostly in the past year. Like *lazy dreams* before it, I submitted it to numerous publishers and it was not accepted anywhere. That's a shame, really, because it contains some excellent poems. I promise, though, history will not repeat itself, and it won't take so many years for that one to see the light of day. Stay tuned.

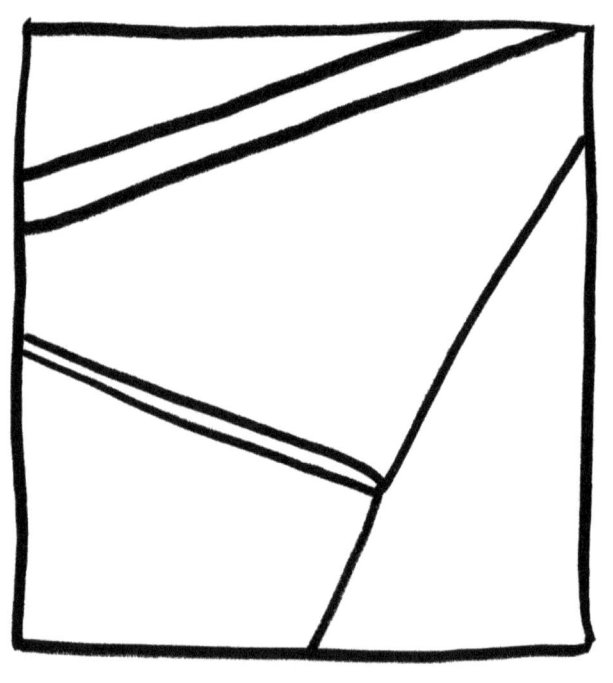

the immeasurable fold (2008)

the pain of walking away
is a coarse thread slowly unraveled
illuminating pain

i've walked away too many times
from too many places, people, things
lovers said and gone, friends forgotten

swift memories fade like the breeze
but the sting of this sorrow
lingers steady and heavy

the prospect of time is daunting
burdened and sincere
that lackluster embrace sooner or later

for we all must face the end
our callused longing
and failed expectation

but this is it
–here, now–
this is everything

it all begins from this moment
immeasurable joy pressed flat
against every sorrow

this synthesis of feeling and prolonged
reaction for the immeasurable fold:
oh if i were so bold

yes, if i were so bold

execution (2000)

we sat in that old chair
in the back living room.
my mother, my comforter
held me in protection
and kept me from life's cruelty.
rounder was there too:
boysbestfriendforever.
i covered my ears
to block the sound of the shotgun;
rounder whimpered.
mom held me; i cried.
dad was outside
helping see to the dirty deed.
it was sarge—grannie's dog—
who was up for execution.
he had committed no crime.

no treason in his blood.
seizure. epilepsy. foaming mouth.
he just wouldn't come out.
that's why we hid inside:
mom and rounder and me.
that's why we cried:
sarge's execution.

spelunking (2000)

i used to go spelunking
with me and my love.
we crawled into pettyjohn's cave
and fumbled in the dark,
flashlights to lead the way.

spelunking is an act of trust,
greeting danger in the dark
then pushing it with a thrust
when you yourself and i
could fall to a dreary death.

in a cave your breath
hangs over your body like a shadow;
intense, fervent, loud.
winged up bats hang at your head
and sometimes make for nightfall.

pettyjohn's cave was muddy,
wet and watered soil.
we pulled out of there one time
all covered head to toe—
we had no clothes to change.

so we stripped down to our underwear
(manly men we were)
and drove back through town towards home.
oh how far i could have gone
in his body, his beautiful cave.

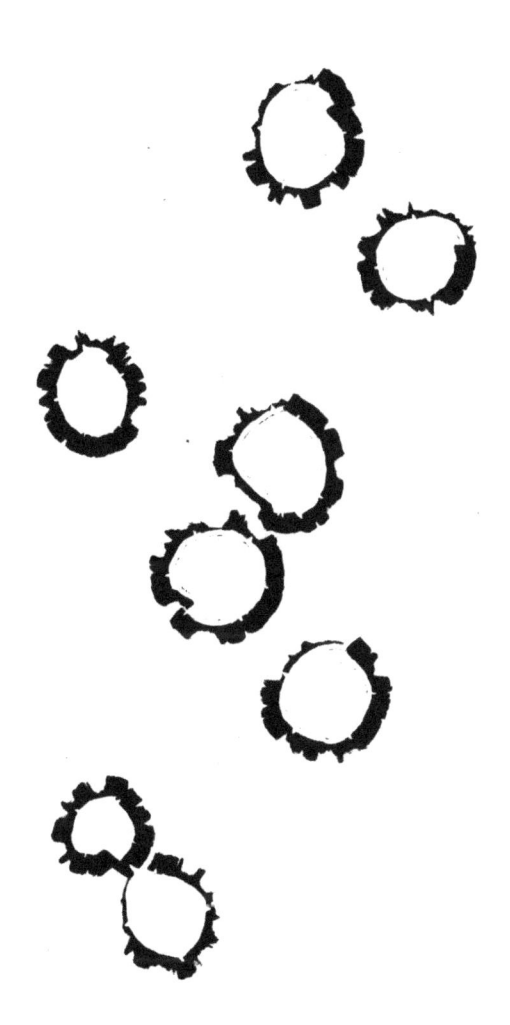

old clothes (2000)

i like old clothes

especially those
my grandmother made

and my father wore
back in the seventies

i like old clothes

they make me feel close
to home

made with hands
like my own

i like old clothes

ode to my roots (2000)

back home on the farm
we never woke up with alarms:
the sun and moon were our guides.

we never tried to hide
from nature, the earth around us.
we never denied

the order of things which are.
and e're i go near or far,
in my heart i am there

always only a step away
from that old, dusty place
where i spent my childhood

mowing the lawn
and hoeing the garden
and keeping the farm.

yes, even in this city
i have never forgotten my roots.
and i know i never will.

my soul is like a garden to till,
waiting to be turned up,
refreshed to my beauty.

but love is my duty,
my sole and solemn promise
and for now it has bound

me to this island of stone.
yes, i call it home,
for home is where you live

and where you belong.
but oh for what i'd give
for a bit of earth under these feet

to walk down west 4th street,
to the farm and back.
but let me pay my duties

and rest in this place
and when i am called onward
i will pick up and go to the other side

without question,
without malice,
without a single doubt of who i am.

tempest (2000)

the rain poured against the earth
like heavy sheets of black velvet
and we rode through the darkness
against the tempest of that night.

the manic rage of insomnia
shrieked against the pavement
and as we rolled into the hospital
our arms trembled, broke apart.

papa's body lay there, skin loose
and heavy hanging, mouth like a cave,
eyes like craters. resting.
gone away. another place.

and our eyes pounded against the floor
like heavy sheets of black velvet
while papa rode through the darkness
towards the tempest of the light.

mary (2004)

mary, go to your garden:
there are flowers there
from seeds you planted
seasons ago, with care

and the food you grew,
tended daily with honest work,
your bonnet tipped towards the sun
to keep out the burning light

while through the night
i rested soundly in the next room
sometimes sitting up late to read,
sure to be quiet so not to wake you

mary, go to your garden:
there are flowers there
from seeds you planted
seasons ago, with care

i can only imagine
what your life was like
through the troubled decades,
two world wars and endless battles

and never mind the hassle
of raising four children,
tending to a husband who
would scarce hear a word you said

and now here you are
fragile as spinning glass,
unable to walk about;
immobile yet still noble

mary, go to your garden:
there are flowers there
from seeds you planted
seasons ago, with care

and now the cross you bear
is heavy like a load of bricks
weighing down upon your soul
waiting for the tock to tick

for the alarm to chime
for the sound of "welcome home"
as your body is released
and your soul is free

mary, go to your garden:
there are flowers there
and you can leave
your cross among them

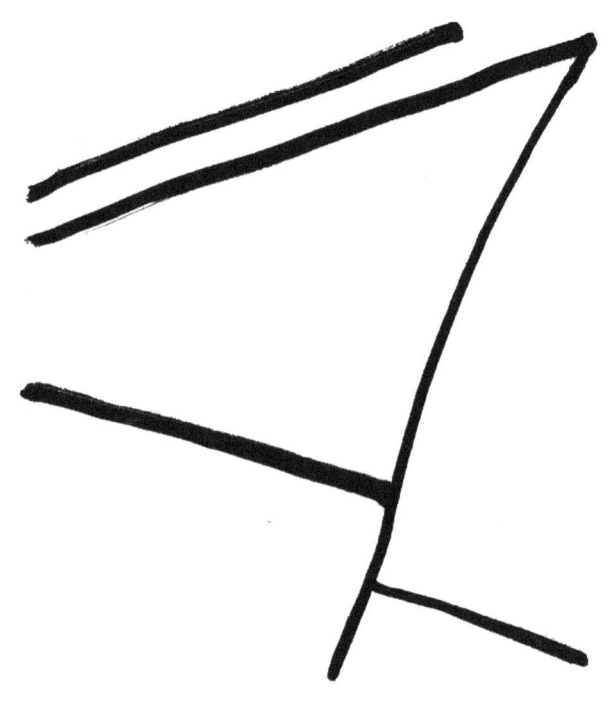

marie was an artist (2015)

she painted pictures
florals and landscapes
and images of the countryside

a quiet scene
stream flowing
through afternoon forest

in the style of bob ross
paint upon canvas
brush stroke and sky

laundry out to dry
a country cabin
smoke rising from chimney

a rural memory
of time forgotten
or maybe only imagined

magnolia blossoms
several arrangements of roses
a teapot of black-eyed susans

a duck in flight
on a calm blue lake
twisted cattails in the shallows

like human bodies
only here for a time
before we pass

she never expected cancer
but it appeared anyway
there among

a dangling strand of fruit
peaches pears and apples
tipped by strawberries

clematis clings to fence posts
where bluebirds rest
waiting to fly home

consider the seasons
trees watching their nakedness
in an autumn lake

when she became sick
everyone knew
where things were headed

a house in the woods
covered in snow
and the silence of winter

a black rabbit
hiding in a basket
but not forgotten

lament over home (2000)

we sat in the kitchen:
it as dirty as the rest of the house.
she peeled potatoes;
i sat in a chair.

we talked about our lives
and the things longfargone
now separated by so many miles.
she stayed close to home;
i went to new york.

i don't blame her for that.
there's a certain poor comfort
about this town lost in the past.
it's just that i could never last.

sometimes i would like to come here,
buy a house, live on serenity.
sometimes i'd like to have my own
front porch to sit on at 4am.
lazyfrontporchblues.

having a hammock outside is nice,
a house with several rooms.
but something about new york
just won't let me leave.

it's a demanding city, that's for sure,
calling me home always so swift.
it's a curse and it's a gift.
sometimes i miss the quietsouthernair,
especially lazy as it is t'night.

i just can't tear my heart from new york city.
no, not yet. but will i ever?
will i ever have the freedom from it?
funny how home's your home.

moment (2000/2013)

if you want to know what life is,
i don't know what to tell you.
the answer's not in this city
or any other place i've been.
except maybe bell buckle tennessee
or new smyrna beach florida.

i haven't been to new smyrna in years
and bell buckle even longer!
though i'd like to visit again:
very nice places.
i don't recall the faces.
i never knew anybody there.
i just knew the earth.

bell buckle was quiet
a wide spot in the road
with about a million antique stores.
it was like rummaging through grandma's attic.
that's another place you might find
just what life is: in the attic.

new smyrna was my home
not home growing up.
it seems like i was born there.
when you get down
far south as new smyrna
the people start growing older
and lived most their lives up north.
no, in the north you won't find answers,
but you may find answers in the old.

i've learned secrets never told
and hearts who've never sang.
isn't that a shame?
no, not really, when you think about it.
you can't stop a heart from singing.
sometimes you may not hear it
but by god i know it's there.
everywhere.

villanow: home.
my georgia paradise.
i never found answers there
but i return often if only in my mind,
those green fields and dewy mornings,
the old swimming hole, the ancient trees,
that fertile valley, the messy red clay
caked between my fingers

yet the question lingers:

and if you want to know what life is,
i don't know what to tell you.

cherokee hills (2013)

was there ever a time
when the land was not scarred
our thoughts marred with violence passed
down by each generation?

did those cherokee hills
leave a river of blood
memory dredged in mud too dark for memory
and lost in translation?

when i think of home
there is joy but deep pain
and it's still the same all these miles back
with time running against you

now when do i go
this solemn exile, this trail of tears
so many years since i have been one
with that land. what are you to me?

when i look back i see
my dimming past ever more,
recollection is sore but no one else recalls
the cross i bear

it is mine alone
and no matter where i tarry
i always carry the sadness of the place
i call home

those cherokee hills
bear the soul of my name—
my heart is lame—my love in exile
set upon the path for a new tomorrow

for a pale horizon
a time soon forgotten fading fast
tradition passed down and slowing
like the decay of a quiet eruption

confederate rose (2015)

a confederate rose grows on the farm
where mother tends to memories like flowers
and stories grow forth from the land:

ancestors gaze—watching—
wondering about our ways
and why it is so hard to remember

we are the same
no matter our name, time, place
no matter the face

looking back in the mirror
faded portraits
hanging on the wall

family bible with litanies of names
born, baptized, married, and died;
so many tears cried:

the land beneath our feet
soaked with cherokee blood
and traditions of isolation

did anyone make amends?
did anyone ask forgiveness
for our sins?

the red clay bunches up between my toes
and i wash my feet in the stream
at the old swimming hole where we were baptized

and cousins crept across the log
dangling bare feet into water
the cool touch of the creek

if you listen, the trees will speak
and everywhere—all around you—
there is a presence

down the way, up the hill
in the barn, through the fields
where a confederate rose grows on the farm

and we grow forth from the land

love in the mourning (2012)

love is love
even if you do not want to hear it

you can exclude, ignore
you can rewrite his story
you can lie and cajole
out of selfish reasons

but love is selfless

love will always be there
even unspoken

love embraces every part of his brother
even the parts he is uncomfortable with
love embraces the difficult pain of loving
and perseveres through the pain

love seeks no special privilege
or desires no special position over others
love knows no rule or law you must keep

love is open to all love
even that which it does not understand

i stand alone this mourning

i have learned to live in the face of abuse
and my heart breaks

love knows a broken heart very well
all too well

love has broken my heart
and i reach out
looking for the pieces

i reach into the void before me
an open hand, vulnerable
i look to faces where there should be love
to mouths who are quick to utter the name of love

and i cannot find love among them

but here i sit
an open hand, vulnerable
arm outstretched
and offer my love

there is a sharp piercing
and i pull my hand back
bleeding

i suck from the wound
this taste of pain
coming into my body
like blood into wine
a flood of memories

i do not bandage the wound
but cautiously
reach out to you again in love
i offer the pain of love

in my mourning
i offer the pain

i offer what you cannot give
for i know the chains in which you are bound

but i also know that love can break them
if only you, too, will ride the pain

yet you are afraid of that pain
unwilling to embrace the pain of love

you are unable to break free
and stand with me in love

but when that day dawns
and you choose love
the dew of the mourning
will wash away all our sins

in love.

and i will stand with you

lazy dreams (2000)

out of basic giving
you have received;
thoughts hold on
to lazy dreams

ideals rest high,
morals too,
with every breath
of all you do

your voice
insists on luxury;
though your mind
is full of other things

like a restless bird
on wings you take flight
somewhere between what you say
and what you think

this discourse is shallow,
your body hot,
for your ambivalence
has left you alone

but out of basic giving
you have received;
so you hold on strong
to lazy dreams

ghazal (2003)

life is a journey to god
a solemn quest to know god

i look out the window onto the world
and i see nothing but limitless god

people move like fingertips caressing magic
across the hem of the silk garment of god

in my soul i know we are all the same
we are all reflections of a divine god

water and wave, all are one
we are the surface of a deep structured god

the world is but a sphere, an holy orb
falling through a black hole toward the light of god

and i am all but here, simple and alone
a strand of hair upon the head of god

**the sound
(which is more alarming?)** (2004)

the sound
of delicate wings
or the wail
of a siren:
which is more alarming?

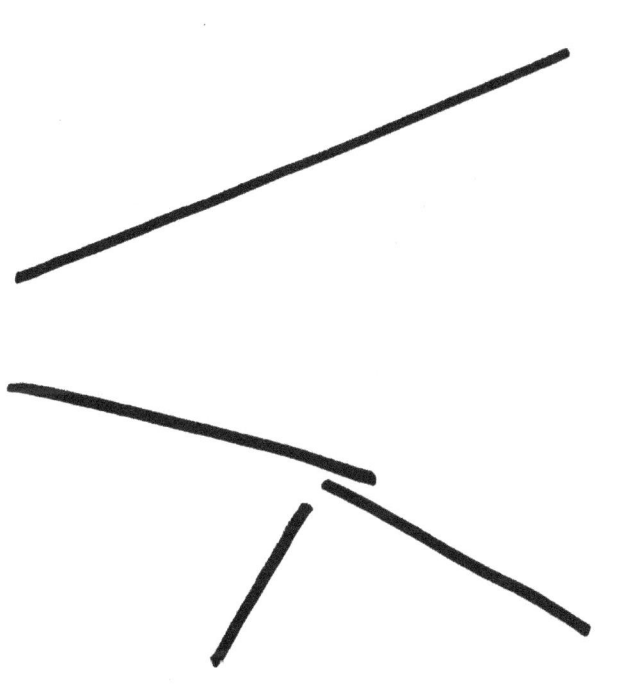

suspension (2003)

i see dead corpses
love is a feral graveyard
drowning in heaven

a lone horse gallops
—quietly—
through my mind

i commit
the symphony of sin
to memory

the sky a photograph
each cloud a tombstone
for dead angels

i find myself sinking
distracted by a sharp pain
that penetrates my side

a pitcher of warm milk
—sits—
on the windowsill

i see dead corpses
love is a feral graveyard
drowning in my glass

sink (2000)

there is a dry spot in me
soaked in dehydration
drowning from exhaustion
dry death in the desert

i have forgotten things
that explain reasons
treasons against one
five days out of seven

it is sucked empty
and inside i am longing
i am begging and hollering
hard for the truth

but dry spots are hidden
they are infectious
and when gone untreated
are a disease to the body

suck in the liquid of life
and wetten your soul
sink to the bottom
of yourself to be whole

08

shadows we shall be (2000)

we are made up of movements:
tiny fragments of verses;
pauses and rests

and yet i forget
you and your shadow
me and my maker

we are all a part of it!
we are woven together,
mended like a quilt

stitch after stilt
the old hand dances
though crippled by arthritis

coming together, colliding,
we move and create sound,
a portrait vividly growing

we move forever around,
our tiny fragments of verses;
pauses and rests

'til so we forget
we are nothing but shadows
and shadows we shall be

detained (2003)

bodies float
like a suspension bridge
through time

i say prayers for the dead
each syllable from my tongue
slender with delight

i omit articles and prepositions
for sake of economy
simplistic language is best

silence echoes against each word
with an odd sound
(though it's the silence that makes it odd)

bodies shift
like an auto changing lanes
on the interstate highway

angel be my guide (2000)

stranger angel
bend down to the earth
and touch me
for all i am
and ever will be

my guardian spirit
left long ago
left my soul broke
and lonely.
bend down and touch me.

bring your eyes
across dark skies
wash your hair in heaven
while i pray for rain.
oh, please stay

stranger angel
and be my guardian!
i am just a simple soul
a small vessel
who needs protection

from the harsh world outside.
angel be my guide.

onewaytripup (2000)

as we grow older
we grow taller, higher,
farther from our roots
and closer to the sky.

we are on a onewaytripup
to a highholyheaven.
it is advised do not look down
if you are afraid of heights.

an angel going by
you know you're not far.
we scrape the sky with our fingers
and the foggy clouds linger.

soon you are enveloped
and the earth has disappeared!
you are going higherhigher
on your newly sprouted wings!

but they're not such disastrous things
as some people think.
there's no gravity in this place
just like outer space!

and we are in an outer
upper clover luck.
we're on the rise yet higher;
on a onewaytripup.

are there? (2001)

there are stories—
too numerous to count—
dancing in my head
with wild abandon

when they are told—
very few and far—
the listening silence
has crippled me

in my giving
has there been taking?
do i give
what is not wanted?

regardless, i have given
and is that enough?
i have hoped
for a lofty dream—

a lazy dream
now fading to vapors
with all the other memories
pages ago

there are stories—
too numerous to count—
dancing in my head
with wild abandon

there are?

heaven's sun so bright   (2000)

in the void of thought against heaven
an angel wedded albatross
flew across the sky
and perched on a horses back

the horse neighed and attacked
the albatross, the pestered prey
and up and stole his wings

so now a highest horse head sings
all through the sky
praising praising heaven!

what do wingless birds do
when they are grounded, clipped,
stranded lonely
just outside kingdom's gates?

they praise!
praise praise praise
just like as though they had wings

they make a song to a maker
asking not why horses fly
asking not why they are not blessed

they dig into clouds
claws
sinking deep within
the outer earthen sky

and soon those horses
hard up for companionship
take the birds on their back,

fill up love in a sack
flight praise praise
through all the night

and hold up heaven's sun so bright
and hold up heaven's sun so bright

when the zephyr came a'calling (2000)

when the zephyr came a'calling
i up and went its way,
out on the breeze a gentle wind
i found my love today

then on a cloud i flew up high
and soared against the air
and on a cloud i touched the sky
then landed on the ground

then when the zephyr came a'calling
out on the breeze a gentle wind,
part of the sky i have become
and will never go back again

cold congregation (2004)

the need for atonement is immense
and your silent recompense
is inadequate

you've gone to battle with
all the freaks and whores
all the restless bores

you've marched against love
in the name of god
for a purpose you call religion

but tell me what's with this
your thoughtless abandon
of ceremony and grace

and how you show your face
is a mystery to me
the way you flaunt hatred

the question of god—of life—
i make no claim
but whether you do or you might

whether you love or you fight
there will be no peaceful amends
for such a cold congregation

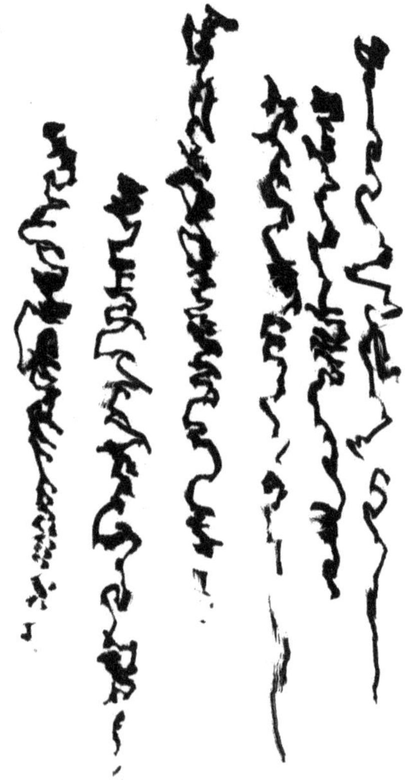

ascension (2003)

this apparent temperament
this lack of joy
all-encompassing grief
fettered defeat
and so on and so forth

i have lost the will
the forlorn joy of my youth
the scattered light
of a thousand stars—bursting—
with determination

cold hesitation
is less and less
the virtue—only vice—
can be true
for the lost and depraved

for the last and the brave
i offer this prayer
that love may be there
even if faintly
and so it is

forever the saintly
praise gods and angels
forever the same
always it is—gently—
one world; one—

one in the same—
the sinner; the saint
all creation lives
—and dies—
without thought or recompense

for all the sins
for all the midnight fucks
—all the stops—
we gather over our grave
to offer useless eulogies

whether they are dead or not
whether life has ceased and stopped
the body, the corpse;
the spirit, the soul
can it rest down in that hole?

a dark cavern
an empty tomb—risen—
is it the third day?
no, yet more a few hours
yet more a few prayers

finally—i am rested—
and have accepted this imminent death
when life shall end
and i ascend
beyond the clouds

into heaven's dark ravine

the agony of betrayal (2006)

horses ride through 'til dawn
and break out in the morning
falling down, gracing god
all through the blackened night

but the killer was alright
and betrayal seemed not dim,
for wits were winning way
and woe was unfulfilling

so they ride—they will not gallop—
forever towards the dawn
and then they see it must be done
to take the shadows home

but by the killer's blade
a knife so shiny sword
he came forthright to that place
to apprehend the lord

of all the horses, all the men
to free the world of all the sin
the horse must die and leave behind
his body there for us to find

his body there for us to find

battlefields (2012)

dreams. wishes. hopes.
float through my head
in cerebellum fits
of fantastic waxing

thoughts are made
—constructed—
with ever such
precision
as skyscrapers and ocean liners;

the architecture of god
is a faint spirit
floating over battlefields
where ancestors tread
in dreams of fallen lovers,
angel dust at their feet

life is delicate;
memory is difficult

here and now
—connected—
the sound of manhattan rain
falls outside my window

these streets, too, like battlefields
strewn with desire:
hopes. wishes. dreams.

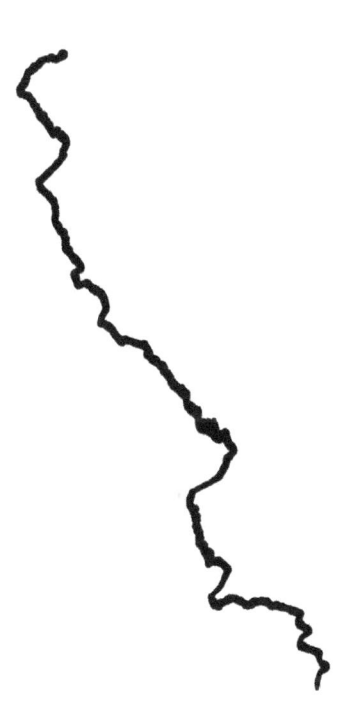

autoatomicanxiety (2004)

the fear of bliss
is an immense
temptation

isolation is a struggle
against the odds of
extinction

where every distinction
between humans and lower
primates

between man and the apes
becomes blurred and
unclear

a disease of social disability
impolite civility and
death

every step every breath
an accomplishment a
triumph

immense and defiant
the world is plagued
diseased

loud detonation
from the mountains to the seas
everywhere

on land and on air
no place no one is
denied

the depths of disguise
the stoic dysfunction of
autoatomicanxiety

death and propriety
the slow release into
atmosphere

yes—it is here—
this deadly urge for
recompense

and the fear of this
is an immense
temptation

**sad american night
(for Jack Kerouac)** (2001)

o sad american night!
blaze right through
to the light
of another dawn
across the ocean!

o sad american night!
i rest under your moon
a lazy croon
and a tired sway
forgotten tomorrow!

o sad american night!
with howling dreams
i forgot
the taste of your air,
the smell of your dew.

o sad american night!
take me back away
and through the light
across your land
towards home!

o sad american night!
cry your tears
and wipe them dry
for such wild emotion
is no stranger here!

o sad american night!
sad, sad
and lonely night
of broken purity
and boundless love!

oh sad american night!
you rest on my shoulders
turning right
all the day made wrong
and fearful!

o sad american night!
you are not the end
but only the start
of a glorious
new beginning!

forever (2011)

your rococo eyes fondle me
across the small of my back
reaching out a sensual touch
stretched nude across wrinkled sheets

i listen to the sound of your breath
the touch of your breathing
the hands of a man to protect
the gentle hands of a man to pleasure

adonai, hear my prayer
ever know my heart is tied to thy hand:
if you bring love i shall serve it
if you bring war i shall fight it

and if you pull my lips toward your body
my tongue shall seek those places
where only the most sacred have tread
and relish the taste of your glory

for thine is the kingdom
and the power
forever

have and have not (2011)

the upward movement accompaniment
swelling emotion orchestrated grace
and the subtle shifting lilt of abundance
barely brought to tip of tongue

that effervescent glowing aura
timid and incalculable almost impossible
for the hidden discourse of desire
and the bold intelligence of love

hold this position cautiously
for the heart is fragile and weeping
cold and arrhythmic fortune sensuous kiss
melting between the sheets of have and have not

falling sweetly upon (2001)

i always felt the mingling of truth
dangle softly between my legs
the curved shape of a hand tingling my thighs
moving upward gently clasping my balls

tugging softly at my skin for love.
i knew the sanctity of such pleasure
and how every god must have lounged
legs open to the universe

in that very moment of creation.
this majestic intercourse is cosmic
and the bliss of life comes and goes
in quiet euphoric moments melting soft as snow

falling sweetly upon your tender skin.

precipice (2011)

the mind is restless
full of hyperbolic thought
stretched out, massaged
punctured with attention
beyond the boundaries set here

this causes a tension
a struggle for freedom
bound with shackles
invisible but literal
and no less limiting

stuck in the middle
the conflict escalates
balance dangled
memory dredged
where thought is a precipice

stay away from the edge

the causes of civilization (2014)

we fight idol minds
to carry forth the work
and the causes of civilization

we break bread
over future generations
yet claw at her like vultures

we rip at her bowels
singed with our own ashes, flooded with decay
but say the causes are unknown

we do not take responsibility
yet we must take responsibility
before it eats us alive

we are but prey
to our own medicine
sipped through intravenous tubes

that have come together—fused—
choking our grip
settled deep in our stomach a regret

we did not fight.
we did not carry forth the work.
and for this—

the indolent yearning of the everyday

vigil and bold (2000)

i have seen the end
of dark tunnels
where the forgotten mouth
is dim with recollection
of a light
of a burning candle
vigil and bold
to guide the weary
and lead the oppressed
through a mire of madness
and unknown fears

i have buried my head
in the ground
where the stench of death
is so strong
that a light
or a burning candle
vigil and bold
could never warm
or bring a kind thought
into the mind
of humanity

i have heard the sound
of howling moons
where starving men
are screaming
in hysterical patterns
of naked flesh
vigil and bold
pressed flat
against the chest
of a stinking corpse
in your attic

i have dug the deepest graves
in the ground
where maggots feed
on the departed
so that even the restful
may rest no more
vigil and bold
against the earth
wrenched in sadness
a mire of madness
and unknown fears

everlasting (2002)

horror lacking—
i forget the reason—
was there ever one?

a giant winged insect
wraps itself around
—what a strong grip—

his hair flipped
like a pacific tsunami—
violent, strict

firm in the grasp
—strong arms—
lost in love

and 1940's nostalgia
of romantic poetry
and high camp

i falter; i faint:
adored like sibyl vane,
to adore

marked by ashes—
stroke—stroke—
i follow down

wrap my arms
around your hands
—do you feel it?—

trapped inside your cocoon—
weaved warmly—
soaked with dew

worn by the passage
from my mouth
to yours

in the everlasting
—alarm—
of love

carried (2000)

with love strapped on my back
and joy waxed on my soles,
i tread across the wilderness
in search of destiny's fate

as would be of late
my mind melds deeper with thought
and memories are like dreams; visions
of rapture and grace overwhelm

onward i bound
across the perils of pride, pity;
onward i stride
through ravines and dark caverns

as nature spreads before me
i sit on the pews of rotten logs,
listen to spellbinding tales,
and bow before boundless love

as below, so above
i have emptied my sack, standing nude
against the air, realizing my journey
was never the hike i had thought

it is truth which i sought
and so now i see:
it was never i who carried love;
love carried me

the waking (2011)

the waking is slow and steady
a subtle shift
a gradual pull
teetering on the edge

the sound is alarming
the thought disarming
a silent brigade
hidden within the walls

the flesh gathers
malleable like clay
with a soft rising
and a tendency to retire

theodora (2011)

the skin is slick with heat
the air so still
my breath is like a rush of wind

i dream of springtime in byzantium
a calm melody floats nearby
while chapels glisten with vivid mosaic

each step a calm patter
i draw out each measure
shuffling my weight about

the delicate dance
of nature awakening
is a bold meditation

the roots of plants
though unseen
are vital to photosynthesis

the soil is rich with moisture
beyond the grasp of my thirst
and unquenched desire

love travels yet higher
through ancient highways
all roads lead to rome

to desolate angels
born on crimson wing
weeping

to spring breezes
shattered with crystal memory
falling

to quiet moments
given for thoughtful prayer
calling

beyond the stars
and holy corridors
i have traveled

and here i am before your throne
kneeling at your feet
a servant bid farewell

this awareness
this eternal mind
is everywhere

i am that
i am nothing
i am everything

though the body may be frail
i seek a calm place
of silent refuge

i seek a place for all seasons
where i may live out my days
calling to you

and waiting for an answer

finished   (2000)

i heard the war of madness
rage across the years
and every beat, every measure
counted it out
every thought so clear

i knew the trial of disposition
had taken its place abroad
and every breath, every word
let it out
and beat the hammer hard

i felt the end of all existence
as day and night diminished
and every light, every bright
burned it out
so everything was finished

about the poems and drawings

"moment" originally appeared in the online journal *Red Truck Review: A Journal of Southern Literature and Culture*, Mar 2014.

Other poems originally appeared in the following various publications by bd-studios.com:

"autoatomicanxiety" and "cold congregation" originally appeared in *let us prey* (2005), a very limited edition/out-of-print chapbook.

The following poems were originally published in *lazy dreams and other memories* (2006), a very limited edition/out-of-print chapbook and exhibition catalog: "the agony of betrayal," "angel be my guide," "are there?," "ascension," "detained," "finished," "ghazal," "heaven's sun so bright," "lazy dreams," "shadows we shall be," "the sound (which is more alarming?)," and "suspension."

"mary" originally appeared in *Jordan's Journey* (2012, written as Jordan M. Scoggins).

"cherokee hills" originally appeared in *INTERSECTION* (2014).

"marie was an artist" originally appeared in a handmade zine of the same name (2015).

The marker-on-paper drawings were made in 2000, the same year as the original manuscript this book is based on, though the drawings were not originally part of that project. This is the first time they have been published.

about the artist

luke kurtis is a Georgia-born interdisciplinary artist. His books include *INTERSECTION*, *The Language of History*, *Angkor Wat*, and *Georgia Dusk* (with Dudgrick Bevins), all part of an ongoing series that combines photography, writing, and design. *obscure mechanics* is his debut full length album of experimental music, originally released in 2008 but reissued alongside this book. He also makes short films, including *the woods are watching* and *convergence*, both documenting his installation art projects of the same names. He lives and works in New York City's Greenwich Village.

also by luke kurtis

Angkor Wat

Georgia Dusk (with Dudgrick Bevins)

INTERSECTION

The Language of History

also published by bd-studios.com

Tentative Armor by Michael Harren

Visions of the Beyond by Stefanie Masciandaro

Puertas Españolas by Josemaria Mejorada & May Gañán

Jordan's Journey by Jordan M. Scoggins

Just One More by Jonathan David Smyth

Retrospective by Michael Tice

www.ingramcontent.com/pod-product-compliance
Lightning Source LLC
Chambersburg PA
CBHW051600010526
44118CB00023B/2770